CABINET OFFICE

OFFICE of the MINISTER for the CIVIL SERVICE

Getting the best out of PEOPLE

A guide to improving communication and involvement at work based on experience in government

London Her Majesty's Stationery Office

© *Crown copyright 1987*
First published 1987

ISBN 0 11 430024 0

contents

foreword

Like many other parts of the public and private sectors the Civil Service has been going through a period of radical change which has often been difficult to accomplish and even painful. Management methods and attitudes have had to alter fundamentally to help cope with this change. And the need to manage change successfully will continue for the foreseeable future.

At the same time, the expectations of staff have been changing: civil servants, like other employees, now expect both to get more out of and to contribute more to their work. They increasingly want to be told about what is going on and be involved and actively participate in achieving goals and priorities.

It has therefore become all the more important that managers in the Civil Service learn and use good communication skills and seek to involve their staff more closely in decisions affecting their work.

The case studies from government departments and the quotations from other sources in this book offer examples of what can be achieved by managers at all levels of an organisation. However, it is the responsibility of senior management in government departments to set the right climate and to make sure that the organisation has the proper machinery for good communications so that the ideas and skills of people at all levels can be properly used.

Junior managers too can, I hope, pick up useful ideas from reading the case studies. As the introductory chapter says, good management is largely commonsense. If you tell people what is happening and why, what is expected from them and what the problems are, you are more likely to get their co-operation and to have them put forward their ideas for improvement.

It would be idle to pretend that in a hierarchical organisation such as a government department attitudes and ways of working are going to change overnight. But the examples in this book show what can be achieved both on the grand scale throughout a large department and on quite a small scale in a single office or establishment. It is I think encouraging that there is such a range of highly successful activity in the fields of communication and involvement. But there is clearly great scope for further improvement, and I hope this book will help in providing a stimulus.

People are by far the most important resource in any government department. There is no shortage of talent and good ideas among civil servants at all levels; it is our job as managers to make sure that those talents are encouraged and used as fully as possible.

Anne Mueller CB

1 what this book is about

*'Management is the art of getting work done
through people.'*

GUIDE FOR NEW MANAGERS

This book looks at ways managers can help to motivate staff by (i) involving them in the organisation of their work and in the management of change and (ii) improving communication between different levels of management and staff.

The largest and most important part of the book, chapter III, consists of examples of approaches that organisations have tried and found practical in making work more effective and rewarding.

Nearly all the examples come from government departments. A few quotations or statements of policy from other employers in the public and private sectors are scattered throughout the book. Much of what is contained in the case studies and quotations seems like commonsense, which is indeed the essence of good management, but it is surprising how rarely in practice it is the first thing to be applied. The examples themselves can give only a brief idea of the circumstances and the techniques: but chapter V gives a list of departmental contacts willing to explain in more detail the aim of the initiative, the methods and resources used, and the outcome.

Chapter II explores some of the issues involved in 'motivation'. There are some brief definitions you may find helpful. But, above all, look at the examples and think how they might apply within your own department, or local office.

the wider picture

'The great change in our society, and a long overdue one, is that it is totally impossible to achieve anything in industry without the freely given collaboration of all people in the organisation. The job of the manager is to enlist that collaboration, and a primary role of the personnel department is to equip the manager with the skills, the systems, and the stimuli to manage the process.'

Sir John Harvey-Jones, Chairman, ICI, writing in *Personnel Management,* September 1982.

management sets the tone

The benefits of greater employee involvement have been widely discussed. For many well-known and successful British companies, there is nothing new in the idea that involving staff at all levels increases productivity and job satisfaction. Many such companies publish their philosophies or statements of company values in employee handbooks or other documents issued to staff. While fine words do not necessarily mean fine actions in practice, the open commitment to a particular style of management helps set a tone and approach for many within the organisation.

Since 1982 there has been a statutory obligation on all British companies employing more than 250 people to disclose, in their directors' reports, action taken during the year to introduce, maintain, or develop arrangements aimed at:

- providing employees with information;
- consulting them regularly;
- encouraging their involvement in the company's performance;
- achieving an awareness of the financial and economic factors affecting the performance of the company.

employee involvement — a voluntary approach

Apart from anything else, involvement is an efficient way to do business, promoting employee loyalty and motivation by making full use of talents and increasing job satisfaction. It is Government policy to encourage this involvement on a voluntary basis. This is essential for three reasons: the variety of working practice prevailing in different companies; *imposing* involvement would not work; and legislation would undermine managerial authority.

a code of practice

Employers' organisations and trades unions have generally welcomed the idea of more participative management. A useful statement of what employee involvement is all about is the joint code of practice drawn up by the Industrial Participation Association (IPA) and the Institute of Personnel Management (IPM) (see page 62). That code, endorsed by the Government, sees the primary aim of employee involvement in managerial terms: securing employee commitment, serving customers better, helping to bring about change. It is also seen as increasing job satisfaction and allowing employees to influence decisions affecting their jobs.

When the IPA and IPM developed the Code they believed that it should cover all employees, in every kind of organisation. Initially it was seen as being most relevant in the private sector but increasingly those working in national and local government have recognised that, making allowances for particular circumstances, the Code is equally relevant for them.

Some differences of emphasis may be called for. For example, in government, the organisation's objectives must recognise statutory responsibilities, and accountability to an elected body — whether Parliament or local authority. The position of customers can also be less straightforward than in the private sector. Customers of a government organisation may be the beneficiaries of a service, or the people who pay for it, or both. In any case, the relationship of customer and organisation is just as crucial as in the case of a commercial undertaking.

summary

- Employee involvement can apply to all employees in any kind of organisation.
- There are many different ways of developing and applying principles.
- Management must take the lead, but involvement is best developed by agreement — with trades union co-operation, where TUs are recognised.
- Rights of management to take decisions and rights of employees and of the TUs under employment law are not threatened.
- Involvement takes training.

what does the organisation get out of it?

Improving communications and devising ways of involving employees in the work of the organisation take time and money; what benefits can be set against those costs? It is always difficult to isolate the impact of any one factor on an organisation's performance; there is evidence, however, from many organisations that a participative management style increases job satisfaction, frequently improves productivity, output, profitability, quality of product or service, and reduces absenteeism and turnover of staff.

For example, a study* of the John Lewis Partnership, which has a long history of employee involvement, concluded that: 'a ... firm which provides a significant voice for all employees, and distributes profits equitably amongst all workers, is not an obstacle to productivity and growth. On the contrary, data suggest that performance might be improved by such ... arrangements'.

A number of other British companies, ranging from Bejam to British Airways, from Rank Xerox to Jaguar, have linked improvements in their performance with participation. Employee involvement can show particular benefits at times of change, for example, the introduction of new technology. The Job Satisfaction project in the National Health Service Central Register at Southport (see page 52) resulted in an increase in productivity, a better service to customers plus more pride in the job and job satisfaction.

Research studies from the USA and other countries carry the same messages: increased employee involvement pays dividends in staff attitude and can contribute to better performance.

'What are the basics of managerial success? Two of the most important are pride in one's organisation and enthusiasm for its works.'

Peters and Austin, *A Passion for Excellence,* Collins 1985.

---

* *The success story of the John Lewis Partnership: a study of comparative performance.* Keith Bradley and Saul Estrin, Partnership Research Ltd, September 1986.

II motivation — a summary of essential issues

'People, once their imagination is fired and they have harnessed their talents, are capable of far more sensitive responses and subtle creations than the most ingenious computer: at the same time, if they are badly treated, the variety and depth of their recalcitrance is tremendous.'

Sir William Armstrong, Head of the Home Civil Service, 1970.

Talking about 'motivation' provokes the obvious response that the matter is quite simple; people come to work because they need to earn money. Most of us would agree. But if we rephrase that truism as 'the only reason civil servants work is the money' most of us would quibble. To quote from an Administrative Assistant interviewed in a recent Job Satisfaction Video:*

'I think the prime factor in going to work is to earn money to keep your family and yourself. That's what you go to work for: to earn a living. But I think, in addition to that, you want the satisfaction that you have done something worthwhile, contributed to your country's welfare in some small measure; not necessarily in a big way, but somewhere that you have done something. I think it's important to every person to feel that they are of use as human beings: we've got to feel useful.'

No one disputes that pay influences people's attitudes to work or that people will protest (actively or passively) at what they see as deficiencies in working conditions or environment. But doing something about attitudes to the work itself calls for action on that work. There's a much stronger expectation that jobs should be satisfying and worthwhile than there was, say, 20 years ago. And in that time there has been another major change in knowledge: about the overriding importance of employees' contribution to the success of organisations; and of how that contribution can be harnessed. This section shows, by summarising the key features, how employee motivation can be influenced positively. These features are:
- the job itself;
- the way work is organised and managed;
- the management of change.

the job itself

No one can decide for others what will 'motivate' them: it is one thing to be told what to do, another that you will like it. But much clearer now are the broad features of jobs likely to result in higher quality of work performance and satisfaction, lower absenteeism, and turnover.

* See page 70.

broad job features essential to high quality of work*

A   Variety of skill and abilities

B   Completing a whole and identifiable piece of work   } leading to   sense of purpose and worth-whileness

C   Impact on the lives or work of other people

D   Job holder has major say in how the job is done   leading to   sense of responsibility

E   Job holder gets direct and clear information about the effectiveness of his/her performance   leading to   sense of achievement from knowledge of job well done/ capacity to modify performance from accurate feedback.

What do these features mean in the Civil Service context? Let's start with the lower grades. In most Civil Service organisations the people in the lower grades are also the 'front line'. That is, they directly provide a service to someone else: a member of the public or another civil servant. To build an effective and satisfying organisation requires, first of all, a vision of what the front line needs. Otherwise there is no means of knowing what management superstructure may be appropriate to support the right way of working at the bottom. Translating the features A–E into a model for Civil Service front line jobs means getting rid of jobs that use only limited skills and replacing them with ones which: combine previously separate tasks in the interests of better service to an *identifiable*

---

* This list of features is based upon one by Hackman and Oldham, quoted in *Motivation and job design*, Robertson and Smith, 1985.

customer; allow for team organisation with scope to influence its own working methods and internal system; enable teams to participate in monitoring their performance, both qualitatively and quantitatively, and in identifying areas for improvement.

Although individual job content is vitally important (features A, B and C), it is not enough. Individual jobs, however well designed, will frustrate rather than motivate if the job holder cannot influence important aspects of the way work is done. In order to have a 'say' (feature D), the individual must work with others to maximise their contribution to efficiency and effectiveness through devising, getting, and using feedback (feature E). To support this kind of working at the front line, we need next to attend to ...

the way work is organised and managed: key needs and aims

INTEGRATION
Between different
functions in the
organisation

TEAM-WORK
Between people in
the organisation

FLEXIBILITY
in response to change

Fast, effective
PROBLEM-SOLVING
making best use of skills and experience

EFFICIENT USE OF RESOURCES
in providing a high quality service

integration is recognising and managing connections between all functions and initiatives. At the front line, this means bringing together different functions affecting the same customer group, so that teams can manage the relationship coherently. At higher levels, it means activity at every level of the organisation has to be tested against its contribution to front-line effectiveness. Thus, for example, the impact of an initiative should be judged by how much it helps the efforts of front-line management.

Quality control measures must be built up from real operational needs, not designed on assumptions about what is supposed to happen. More established functions like personnel management and manpower control must also be re-examined so that line managers can be given the delegated authority they need. Specialists need to operate in support of line managers.

Nowhere is the need for integrated action more pressing than in the design of new office technology, where partnership between IT specialists and line managers is essential. This means substantial effort being put into mutual education so that both can involve front-line staff in the design and development of new systems.

team-work means focussing on the human resources available rather than the formal positions people occupy. At the front line, it means getting people used to working together flexibly and interchangeably so that they willingly contribute their abilities according to the needs of the work. Supervisors and line managers need to demonstrate team-work in practice, continually reassessing their activities and how they are using their expertise to deal with current problems.

This approach implies cutting down on the supervisory functions of successive layers of managers: performance monitoring becomes an integral part of the front-line task of self-improvement. Managers then have more time for problem-solving, improving systems, and coaching to increase front-line teams' effectiveness. It also means the manager's most important activity is keeping in close touch with the needs of front-line staff, so that problems are accurately identified and new systems realistically designed. At higher levels, senior management's priority becomes identifying and removing the obstacles that get in the way of management-as-communication.

flexibility is simply having the confidence, capacity and competence to respond to change. At the front line it means, for example, a readiness to modify individual 'whole jobs', where changes in work or personnel make a different approach more effective because individuals know they are part of a team doing a worthwhile job for a customer. Similarly, it means managers adapting their role as changes progress: for example, from problem-solving to coaching/support to evaluators.

managing the change

Improving the organisation's capacity to change involves developing new ways to release talent and motivate staff. This is particularly important if line managers and front-line staff are to contribute to new office technology systems. The continuing search for more cost-effective procedures and policies also provides opportunities for employee involvement to bring about changes in managing and organising. The key aspects of managing change are:

- stating the organisation's 'mission' clearly, simply, and frankly;
- clarifying and communicating specific objectives, including their relationship to the mission, and evaluation criteria;
- creating design groups — steering groups, co-ordinating groups, and task groups — to bring together people affected;
- preparing design groups to perform their task by helping them with team-work, problem-solving, and education/information;
- making full use of experimentation to test ideas with minimum risk;
- regularly communicating progress, including areas of uncertainty;
- long-term vision: maintaining constancy of purpose through accomplishment of intermediate goals that make sense to participants as contributions to long-term objectives;
- conscious improvement of industrial relations through trades union involvement;
- emphasis on quality in team-work, end-product, and efficient use of resources.

Although different change mechanisms may be appropriate to different organisations, the essentials of mission and end-product are not. The most important job of senior management is to make sense of these and relate them to particular tasks.

Mission and end-product should be simply grounded in quality of service. Thus, in one British public sector organisation, something as straightforward as 'quality, fairness, and caring' is currently proving a highly effective basis for enlisting employee involvement. The prize is quite simple: quality and efficiency in service provision. That is something which makes sense to our Administrative Assistant in the video and restores dignity and purpose to his manager. It is the only viable basis for employee involvement in the Civil Service.

customer service — the key motivator

Customer service (to internal and external customers) is a natural and powerful source of staff commitment to doing a job well. Teams of staff serving a customer-grouping take pride in that service. Commitment to customer service provides a much firmer basis on which to improve efficiency and effectiveness than measures directed solely or primarily at cost-reduction. Customer service within government is not always simply a matter of fulfilling customer needs since some civil servants are employed to regulate as well as help customers, and often there is more than one customer. But front-line staff are well able to understand the complexities and potential conflicts of their work (eg being both helpful and regulating) and to make a major contribution towards resolving them.

Example
Department of Health and Social Security, initiative to improve service to the public

In 1982, the Department of Health and Social Security (DHSS) set out to see how it could improve the service given to customers in local offices. A whole range of possible improvements was listed as being important to the public. They included:
1. the way in which people are dealt with when they come into contact with the Department, and how the Department communicates with them — in person, on the telephone, in writing;

2. the quantity and quality of advice given;
3. the image the Department presents to the world;
4. the way in which information is communicated;
5. making sure the public knows where to get personal advice.

DHSS information leaflets were reviewed; it was agreed that more emphasis should be given to publicising the Department positively in the media. Throughout the initiative priority was given to using the ideas of the staff who were in the front line.

The results ranged from cheap and simple ideas such as placing magazines in public waiting rooms, to a nationwide Freephone service to help the public get general advice on benefits. Furthermore, staff agreed, among other things, to:

- publicise the Department's work by giving talks to voluntary organisations, schools, hospitals, and to staff of local authorities;
- man information stands at exhibitions, to give advice to members of the public;
- drive and man mobile information units in Scotland and Wales, taking advice and information to remote rural areas.

By May 1986, 47% of local offices had appointed an information officer. Overall, junior staff from DHSS local offices produced and implemented dozens of ideas for improving customer service and these were published in a handbook of good practice (see p 69).

what staff say

Meanwhile, two separate attitude surveys within the same department — DHSS — looked at what staff themselves say are the main factors that motivate or demotivate them. The way the surveys were carried out and the main findings are described in chapter III, page 26. 'Doing a job which is worthwhile ... making a positive contribution ... responsibility ... varied work' were typically quoted as factors that motivated middle managers taking part.

'At the moment too many of our workplaces stifle enterprise and initiative. The result is that people go elsewhere — to their pigeon lofts, to their do-it-yourself, to betting shops, where they show far more skill in manipulating numbers than most employers encourage them to show at work.'

Lord Young of Graffham, Secretary of State for Employment, speaking to a NEDO conference, April 1987.

Points to remember

1. State the organisation's mission clearly, simply and frankly.
2. Always bear in mind the overriding importance of employees' contribution to the success of the organisation.
3. Base the 'mission' and end product firmly on quality of service.
4. Encourage customer service as a firm basis for improving efficiency and effectiveness and as a key motivator of staff.
5. Define your customer and what you mean by customer service.
6. Don't sloganise: let front-line staff say how *they* see the service they perform, and work up common objectives with them.
7. Work first on issues that front-line staff identify as hindrances. Put internal organisation or procedures right first.
8. Build confidence in teamwork by providing support and training in effective problem-solving; involve managers and supervisors.
9. Be willing to experiment and test ideas.
10. Build in ways of evaluating change from the beginning and encourage staff to devise feedback measures.
11. Make clear that top management supports the initiative.
12. Discuss the initiative with the local trades unions and seek to enlist their support and ideas.

a short guide to the terminology

One of the problems of employee involvement is the language. With so many 'in' words and phrases around, communication is often difficult

— in fact you might find it a complete turn-off.

This short section describes how some common terms are used. The main thing to remember is that different authors and speakers are likely to use the same expressions to mean different things: it's important to find out exactly what is meant in each context.

Motivation. Psychologists use this term to explain what makes people tick. Nowadays it's widely used to describe people's willingness to work. Beware, however, of vague usage: what exactly is it that a person may or may not feel motivated to do? Thus 'motivating' someone to do something can come across as highly manipulative — the opposite of treating people as if they had minds of their own and the capacity to make informed choices.

Communication — perhaps the most widely abused term. Thus 'failure of communication' is sometimes used to cover up conflict, rather than to describe genuine misunderstanding. A good working definition is 'communication is what happens when a message is understood by the receiver as the sender intended'. It is an active process, which involves listening as much as sending messages. There is an important practical distinction in management communications between methods that are primarily intended to get messages down the organisation and approaches that aim to improve communications in both directions — upwards as well as from the top.

An example of the former is **Cascade Briefing**, which is often used to describe downward communication from senior management to successive levels of staff through a series of **Briefing Groups** — meetings between a line manager and his/her staff for passing information. **Team Briefing** is a systematic cascading system pioneered by the Industrial Society: it is designed to get a message rapidly through the hierarchy.

Employee Involvement (EI) itself is a confusing term. Sometimes it is used for any activity in which the workforce is told or asked about something. In other organisations, however, it goes much further and is used to describe an organised process of participation — involving employees in decision-making.

Quality of Work Life (QWL). This phrase is also used in two ways. One refers to the quality of employee experience at work — what people feel about their jobs. The cther refers to a joint process of organisational improvement (like EI as participation). Management and union formally agree to aims of improved quality and productivity as well as employee well-being, and to the structures and method for workforce participation in achieving them.

Job Satisfaction (JS), similarly, is used in two ways. First, the general meaning, which is simply what people feel about their jobs. The second meaning, specific to the Civil Service, refers to the work of the Cabinet Office (OMCS) Job Satisfaction Team (JST). The JST provides advice on the processes of involving managers and staff to achieve improved service quality, as well as increased job satisfaction — see the example on page 52.

There are various terms used about improving jobs. Fortunately they are fairly precise in their original meaning, if not always in their usage.

Job Rotation is what it sounds like — planned approaches to job change to increase variety and reduce monotony. **Job Enlargement** means building more tasks of a similar level of responsibility into the same job — again, to increase variety and reduce monotony. **Job Enrichment** is increasing the scope for achievement, responsibility, or decision-taking into a job so as to increase opportunities for satisfaction from the fuller use of a person's skills and knowledge.

Job Design is the term often used to describe a participative approach to change in job content. Research has established the broad features of jobs likely to result in improved organisational effectiveness and individual job satisfaction (see page 9).

Another approach that emphasises change in the system as a whole (as opposed to isolated bits) is **Organisational Development (OD)**. Defined as 'seeking to generate valid information that will enable free choices leading to planned organisational change', OD focusses on improving inter-personal skills, trust, and openness to create a climate for sound decision-taking and effective use of human resources. ('OD' is often used loosely to refer to any activity vaguely connected with the human aspects of management.)

'**Groups**' of all kinds crop up in confusing profusion; these are some of the most common terms:

Steering Groups bring key parties together — eg senior management, TU officials — to give authority and direction to a change by planning, co-ordinating, and monitoring.

Problem-Solving Groups are the means of involving the workforce directly in identifying problems and in testing and implementing solutions. These may be based on existing work groups, eg a management team or a section led by a junior manager; or problem-based with representatives drawn from different sections and/or grades.

Quality Circle is often used to describe a voluntary group which has been trained in problem-solving, group working, and presentational skills. They choose their own problems, work out solutions, and present them to management for implementation. This is *not* however an isolated shop-floor technique. It depends for its success on commitment from management to constant improvement of quality through team-work, and management knowledge of problem-solving methods.

Statistical methods — eg, **Statistical Process Control (SPC)** — are now becoming central in advanced approaches to quality improvement at all levels. Basic statistical concepts are used to enable management and shop-floor to identify and remove sources of waste and defects in products and services.

III what is going on?

examples of work from government
departments

introduction

This chapter looks at a variety of examples, from a number of departments, of systems and approaches that have been used to encourage good communication and effective employee involvement. Some are in the early stages of development; others have been in operation for some time and have been adapted and modified as weaknesses in their original design have been spotted. These specific examples illustrate the wide range of systems and approaches which can be used to meet the multitude of situations: formal and informal, large and small, specialist and generalist, organisational and personal. Some of the examples could be relevant to your particular area of work.

In thinking about ways of improving communications or ideas for increasing employee involvement, the main need is to avoid constantly reinventing the wheel. A few words on the telephone or in person with someone in another organisation who has tackled similar problems will be worth many days of working things out from scratch.

Those responsible for the initiatives described in this chapter will be happy to talk to others about how they set about the work, what it cost, what results they got. There is a list of departmental addresses and telephone numbers in chapter V.

1. communication audits and attitude surveys

introduction

How often have you heard colleagues complain about the lack, timing, and nature of communications in your department? Complaints like 'why weren't we told beforehand?'; 'this Office Notice is boring, just lists of people moving about the Department'; 'I haven't got a clue what that Division does, I didn't even know it was part of the same Department'; 'why can't the department let us know before the trades union — or the press — do so?'.

On the other hand, how often have you thrown management newsletters, bulletins etc in the wastepaper bin before reading them, or after giving them just a cursory glance? The chances are that the answer to both questions is 'frequently'. Communications only work when they are effective; poor communications are almost as bad as no communications at all.

This problem has now been recognised in a large number of departments which have looked at existing arrangements for both internal and external communications.

Many departments and other government bodies, from the Ministry of Defence with some 170,000 civilian staff, to the Public Record Office, with only about 400 staff, have carried out surveys, looking at the full range of management and staff communications.

staff views and cost effectiveness

The surveys have varied in a number of significant respects. Some, such as that carried out by the Management and Personnel Office (MPO) of the Cabinet Office, have been primarily aimed at identifying staff views on the effectiveness of existing communications, their weaknesses and strengths, and how they might be changed for the better. Others, such as the Department of the Environment (DOE) scrutiny into dissemination of information outside Government have been more concerned with cost effectiveness or with communications between different parts of the organisation. All have shown that a more positive, organised approach is necessary if communications are to be effective.

Some departments have used their own staff to carry out the surveys, while others have preferred to call in outside experts.

Example
Board of Inland Revenue — communications survey

In 1983 the Board commissioned management consultants, Hay-MSL, to examine its existing internal communications system and to propose ways of creating a greater awareness of (i) management objectives and (ii) corporate identity. Hay-MSL visited and spoke to staff at all levels in headquarters and in local and regional offices in the Taxes, Collection and Valuation Office networks and one non-network office.

Summary of recommendations

1. A statement of communications policy to help line managers do a better communications job.
2. Senior managers should ensure their subordinate managers were able to explain the impact of any change upon staff.
3. Dissemination of information should be better disciplined and the volume of paper reduced.
4. Subordinate managers should be encouraged to talk to staff.
5. Introduction of a quarterly staff magazine and a monthly letter to managers from the Chairman.
6. The establishment of a communications group bringing together press office, publicity unit, and internal communications.
7. A pilot project involving videos.

Implementation

As a result, the Inland Revenue set up a Communications Group with a Head of Communications; published communications policy guidelines; introduced a monthly Chairman's Newsletter about developments in the management field; introduced a quarterly departmental magazine, *Network*; and set up a pilot exercise in the Eastern Counties Region in the use of:

- video;
- quarterly meetings between officers in charge and regional management;
- sending certain HQ papers out fortnightly rather than daily to ten districts, and emphasising better targetting of them by office managers, and distribution at regular face-to-face group meetings.

The Inland Revenue asked Market and Opinion Research International (MORI) to carry out a pair of attitude surveys in 23 Tax Districts in the Eastern Counties Region, in January 1985 and March 1986. This pair of before-and-after or 'book-end' surveys was one way of evaluating the

> pilot exercise described above. The surveys also explored staff's perceptions and attitudes on a wide range of management and communications matters.

Other departments which have carried out communications surveys, either through consultants or using their own resources, include: Cabinet Office (MPO); Department of the Environment; Department of Trade and Industry; Export Credits Guarantee Department; Home Office; Inland Revenue; Ministry of Defence; Manpower Services Commission; National Audit Office; Paymaster General's Office; Public Record Office. Surveys have also been carried out in several parts of DHSS. Cabinet Office (MPO) and Treasury commissioned a survey of communications between those two central Departments and other parts of the Civil Service.

surveys for specific purposes

Communications between headquarters and regional/local offices

The staff of many government departments and bodies — for example, the DHSS and the Manpower Services Commission — are spread throughout the country, working in hundreds of local offices. Staff in these offices often feel that despite the fact that they are at the 'coalface' and actually have to operate the instructions and policy changes from headquarters, their views on the measures and their practicability are never sought.

Physical separation does make communication more difficult in both formal instructions and more general personnel contacts. Both the Inland Revenue and HM Customs and Excise carried out surveys of the written instructions sent out to local offices: as a result instruction books were re-written and training provided in writing new instructions.

> Example
> **Manpower Services Commission — staff communications survey (by the MSC staff)**
>
> In 1985 the MSC Psychological Service

carried out a study of communications between head office and the field network. The study aimed to identify the views of staff on communications and make suggestions how they might be improved.

Fourteen Employment Division and Training Division areas spread throughout the country (covering work in Jobcentres, the Community Programme, the Disablement Advisory Service, Training Programme Assessment etc), spread throughout the country, were involved in the pilot and main surveys carried out by questionnaire. Some 696 staff, covering the grades Administrative Officer (AO) to Area Manager/Area Employment Manager, completed the questionnaire.

The study concluded that a communication gap did exist between Head Office and the field.

recommendations

1. Regional and Area management should be helped to find their own solutions to the problems identified by the survey — first in the four pilot areas then in the ten main areas. These should be reported back to the Chairman's Management Committee as a basis for considering national guidelines.
2. Top management should consider whether they would support fuller field participation.

MSC also carried out an efficiency scrutiny of written communications and centrally prepared instructions, aimed at reducing the volume of paper and improving the effectiveness of internal communications.

house journal surveys

Many departments have introduced new departmental journals; others have radically altered existing ones. Before doing so, many have first commissioned attitude or readership surveys to see whether there was a need for a house journal and what it was that readers expected from it. Once new journals have been introduced, further surveys to assess their impact and success have been commissioned. The Inland Revenue quarterly magazine *Network* was launched as one outcome of the communications survey carried out by Hay-MSL (see page 21). Other departments who have used readership surveys to test the usefulness and attitudes to house journals include DHSS and Department of Trade and Industry (DTI). The Health and Safety Executive carried out a controlled readership survey of its monthly journal 'Compress' by means of telephone canvassing to find out what staff wanted and expected from the journal.

Example
DHSS newspaper, *Window*

Window was launched as the DHSS house newspaper in June 1984, replacing the previous small, black and white glossy magazine sold to a minority of staff. *Window* adopted a radically different style: a newspaper format with coloured photographs and free distribution to all staff.

Plans were made to evaluate the paper after a year's issues by means of a postal survey of staff, to find out the extent to which it was read and what readers thought of it. A representative sample of 3,881 staff was drawn from locations covering about 90% of departmental employment. 68.7% responded: a satisfactory response rate for a postal survey. Overall, three-quarters of respondents said they received their own copy each month. Only 13% said they never read *Window*; 28% read most or all of it. The majority read a few articles (28%) or just glanced through it (31%).

The most widely read items were the cartoons, readers' letters, and articles on current work or new development in offices or branches. But even the weightier articles on departmental objectives and plans were read by 78% at least sometimes.

Certainly staff throughout the department strongly supported the idea of a departmental newspaper. Nearly two-thirds of those who read *Window* said they felt more in touch with what was going on in the department as a result. There was a high level of satisfaction with the style, layout, and range of topics covered, but there was a feeling that the paper took too much account of management's views and that it shied away from controversy. These findings were reported back to staff through an article in *Window*, and a commitment was given to act on the suggestions made.

reviews of office notices

Other departmental surveys, for example in DTI, Cabinet Office (MPO), and MAFF, looked specifically at the style, frequency, and distribution of office notices. In each case changes were made to improve the style, frequency, and format so that the notices would better capture the attention of staff and meet people's needs. Within the Department of Employment Group, the Unemployment Benefit Service carried out communications audits in two regions, scrutinising the effectiveness of office communications by means of questionnaires and interviews.

motivation and attitude surveys

When communications are poor and people do not know or understand what is happening around them, motivation and morale are bad. Other factors — pay, boring work, domestic circumstances — all affect motivation. Attitude surveys not only allow management to see what staff think about communications generally, but can also help identify more general motivation problems or allow management to assess the impact of new measures.

Example
Department of Health and Social Security — attitude surveys

Two separate attitude surveys within DHSS looked at what staff said were the main motivating and demotivating factors. The surveys were carried out within the Department's North Fylde Central Office (NFCO) at Blackpool, which has a staff of around 4,400, and the Newcastle Central Office (NCO) with a staff of some 10,000. The staff at NFCO are mainly occupied with the consideration and payment of claims to War Pensions and several social security benefits, including Attendance and Mobility Allowances and Family Income Supplement. NFCO also deals with superannuation for the NHS, Legal Aid assessment, and various other tasks. NCO records the information needed to pay contributory benefits, such as retirement pensions, and child benefits as well as issuing payments. It is also responsible for various matter relating to the payment of National Insurance contributions. In each case a statistical sample of staff (Executive Officers (EOs) in NCO, EOs and Higher Executive Officer (HEOs) in NFCO) were asked a series of questions about their work, responsibilities, relations with line managers, work loading, promotion, pay, accommodation, and job satisfaction.

Findings

In the case of NCO, it emerged that the top six questions staff thought had the most bearing on their performance and on their attitude to the DHSS were: work quality; promotion prospects; responsibility; pay; communications; morale.

There were similar findings at NFCO, where both the HEOs and EOs indicated that factors motivating people positively were: worthwhile job; contributing towards work of the branch; responsibility; varied and good quality work; involvement in decision making; recognition by line management; good working relations.

The factors that staff in both offices found to be demotivating were: dissatisfaction with pay; the effects of departmental or Government policies; promotion prospects; accommodation and 'staff morale'.

In the case of NCO, the attitude survey was complemented by a separate survey of communications within the office. NFCO have also carried out an attitude survey among clerical and other grades, and a survey of communications is also planned involving a sample of all staff up to Grade 7.

Other departments which have carried out attitude surveys include Manpower Services Commission.

points to remember when setting up a survey

What is the survey attempting to identify? What are the aims of improved communications?

1. **Objectives**
   - Identification of key concerns, attitudes, and needs of staff.
   - A statement of communications policy.
   - Greater staff awareness of the department's role.
   - Greater staff understanding of management objectives.
   - Corporate identity.
   - Improved cost-effectiveness.

2. **Contacts**
   - Consult those in other departments who have been involved in surveys: some contacts are included in chapter V.

3. **Survey team**
   - Appoint a specific individual or team to carry out the survey within a specified period and to a fixed budget. An internal team will know the department and the existing arrangements. External consultants can bring in expertise on surveys and communications and can give better guarantees of confidentiality, anonymity, and independence — but they may be more expensive and have a longer learning curve. Make sure the consultant knows what you want: don't be tempted to buy ready-made attitude surveys.
   - Ensure the survey team know who they are reporting to. Top management should be involved at an early stage, and be seen to be so if the project is to get full support all down the line.

4. **Plan for action**
   - Never begin a survey unless the resources will be available to follow it through. The expense of the survey is likely to be small when compared to the cost of implementing its recommendations. Apart from expenditure on communications—

media, printing, videos etc — there may well be training costs and organisational costs from the establishment of a permanent communications unit or a post of communications officer. A preliminary pilot survey in just one part of the organisation can be an economic way of indicating what a full survey will find, and the possible difficulties.

5. **Feedback**
   - Make sure that those who have taken part in the survey are shown that their views have been taken into account and are told of the survey's outcome. Publish results as openly as possible: a concealed communications survey is a contradiction in terms.

6. **Implementation**
   - Keep the people who have worked on the survey involved in the action team looking after implementation of the recommendations. Rather than a rigidly prescribed plan from the centre, encourage follow-up action by explaining what the survey found and discussing the problems with local managers who must overcome them. Involve managers in arriving at solutions.

7. **Evaluation**
   - If changes are introduced as a result of a survey, check that the desired results have been achieved. Remember that changes take time to introduce: gradual change, often a fairly slow re-education programme for managers, is usually more effective than the introduction of a wide variety of ill thought-out initiatives.

8. **Repetition**
   - A one-off survey gives you only a snapshot at one point in time. Regular surveys tell you whether changes in policies and procedures are having any effect on staff attitudes — the way they think of the organisation and the work they do.

2. organising communications

A new and positive approach to communications cannot be achieved without senior management being strongly committed to the changes. Senior managers are busy people and, even with their support, initiatives are almost bound to fail, unless someone is given responsibility for seeing the initiative through. Nor can this person, or persons, act in isolation from the rest of the department. All of us have a role — managers and managed. We have to charge a specific individual with a particular task in connection with communication or setting up a formal communications team. Management provides a framework on which the rest of us can build. This section looks at examples of these frameworks.

Communications Officers

A number of departments have either appointed a full-time Communications Officer or given the responsibility to a particular officer along with other duties.

Example
Export Credits Guarantee Department (ECGD)

Following a communications survey in 1985, ECGD appointed a Departmental Communications Officer with the following aims:
- oversee all internal communications including publication of the annual report to staff;
- ensure that all communications fit with the Department's general communication strategy;
- review all written communications;
- organise 'key communicator briefing sessions' and the monthly line briefing arrangements.

He reports directly to the Head of Personnel Management.

Communications Committees or Groups

Example
Home Office

In November 1985, the Home Office set up a Standing Group on Communications between management and staff. Its terms of reference were 'to consider what information should be made available to staff by management and the means by which it should be promulgated; to examine specific communications matters put to it from time to time by the Personnel Management Sub-Committee on the Departmental Whitley Council or personnel management divisions, and to make recommendations; and to report to the Personnel Management Sub-Committee from time to time on the Committee's progress'.

The Group's first task was to review the effectiveness of Home Office notices as a means of communicating management messages to staff, and to consider the introduction of a house journal.

Costs are confined to the time of members of the Standing Group. Communications work takes about 25% of the time of a Grade 7 and of an HEO. Other members attend meetings about once a month.

Other departments listed as having carried out communications surveys (see page 20) have given responsibility for management-staff communications either to a single officer, or a communications unit.

identifying key communicators

Good communications depend on continued effort: they cannot be left to *ad hoc* studies nor can the responsibility be left to one individual. Good communications are an integral part of every manager's job. The line manager has an increasingly important role to play. This has been reflected in a number of organisations where senior line managers have been identified as key communicators and given special tasks to perform.

Example
Ministry of Defence (Royal Navy Dockyards)

The two naval dockyards, at Devonport and Rosyth, employ some 18,000 people and have an annual turnover of about £420 million. In July 1985 the Government announced that following a review of naval work it was proposing to introduce legislation to put the dockyards under commercial management. The trade unions were strongly opposed to the move, which made good communications between management and the workforce all the more important. Hay Management Consultants had been called in earlier by the Chief Executive Dockyards in anticipation of significant changes to dockyard operations.

Hay found that the trades unions and local media were considered by the workforce to be a more credible source of information than local management. Existing methods of communicating with the workforce, through monthly dockyard newspapers and a weak cascade briefing system, were not effective enough to support a major programme of change. Hay worked with MOD managers to devise a communications strategy and also helped train thirty key MOD people in media work.

Communications strategy
- All those affected should be properly and promptly informed of the proposals in detail and how they would be affected.
- Dockyard managers should explain the programme of change on managerial grounds.
- MOD must be the prime source of information for all interested parties.
- Arrangements should provide access to information, not just more paper.
- The Dockyard Planning Team should take the lead.

Action
1. The issuing of a ministerial statement followed by a letter to all employees at home.
2. A series of presentations at the yards.
3. The introduction of topical weekly/ fortnightly bulletins — produced in-house on two sides of A4 paper handed to employees by individual managers. Each bulletin takes two man-days per week to produce.

4. Production of 'Annual Reports' at Devonport and Rosyth, setting out operating targets for a two-year period against which progress can be reported quarterly in the local bulletin.

'For an internal communications programme to be effective, everyone concerned must appreciate what the point of the exercise is'.

The Winning Streak Workout Book, Goldsmith and Clutterbuck.

points to remember

1. Don't appoint a Communications Officer or set up a Communications Committee until aims, objectives and workload have been clearly identified.
2. Ensure the person or group concerned:
   - is given a clear job description and objectives;
   - knows to whom they report;
   - knows how they fit into the department's organisational structure, eg vis-a-vis the Press Office;
   - knows the budget within which they are expected to operate.
3. Give the Communications Officer or Committee support by identifying key communicators in line management through whom communications can be transmitted and received.
4. Ensure key communicators know what is expected of them, both generally and in relation to each piece of information they receive.
5. Introduce organisational change during a period of relative calm when rational decisions can be made, not in response to industrial relations crises.

3. improving written communications

In the Civil Service a great deal of communication, both internal and external, is in writing. It is a medium with which civil servants are familiar and comfortable but, perhaps because familiarity breeds contempt, it is an area where the Civil Service has been severely criticised in the past. The 'Plain English'

Campaign has done much to remedy many of the weaknesses, especially in relation to external communications and form design, but there is still a great deal that managers can do to improve things.

Apart from the *quality*, it is worth looking at the *quantity* of written communications; at departmental, divisional or local level, there are ways of staunching the daily flood of paper across desks. It is possible to experiment with ways of targetting paper better: for example, similar items can be grouped together and distributed as bundles or bulletins, with contents clearly flagged or indexed; notices can be saved up for weekly or fortnightly rather than daily distribution. Local managers are in the best position to say what are the essential items of paper, how often they should be distributed, to whom and in what form.

house journals

'Another medium less well used than it might be is the company newspaper. Usually very cheaply and badly produced, it carries a clear visual message of indifferenece when placed next door to the glossy sales literature in the company foyer. It says, "Customers are valued more than employees." '

The Winning Streak Workout Book, Goldsmith and Clutterbuck.

Many government departments and other bodies have house journals, ranging from typewritten newsletters to tabloid newspapers to glossy magazines. Content, frequency, and costs also vary widely because departments have tried, as far as possible, to tailor the style, size and presentation to meet the needs of the audience. Many have carried out surveys to assess staff needs and preferences before making changes. In some cases, journals concentrate on communicating management interests. In others, more is made of social and sports news and events. Some departments put control into the hands of an editorial or advisory board, although day-to-day exercise of editorial judgement normally rests with the editor.

House journals can help to foster a sense of departmental identity, to maintain morale, and to provide an informal channel for communicating management information to staff and for seeking their views on major issues.

Example
Board of Inland Revenue — Network

This quarterly house journal tells all members of staff about the nature, scale and purpose of changes taking place within the Department.

Network is seen as background information, not as an alternative to line managers as a source of news. Production is organised by outside writers, editors, designers and printers under the control of an internal editorial board (chaired by the Permanent Secretary) and an internal managing editor with day-to-day responsibility for the house journal.

The external costs for 76,000 copies are about £96,500 per year (in 1987). A survey in 23 Tax Districts in Eastern Counties Region in March 1986 (by which time five issues of *Network* had appeared) invited staff to say how much of the magazine they read. Two-thirds said that they did more than just glance through it, a level of readership almost identical with the well-established monthly newspaper of the Department's biggest clerical staff union.

Other departments which have launched new house journals, or extensively remodelled old ones, in recent years include: Department of Trade and Industry; Cabinet Office; DHSS; Lord Chancellor's Department; Government Communications Headquarters; Public Record Office; Export Credits Guarantee Department.

newsletters and bulletins

Example
Department of Employment — Group Personnel Unit

To keep staff in touch with personnel developments across this varied group, the Group Personnel Unit (GPU) in Department of Employment headquarters produces two separate but linked newsletters written in a lively and easy-to-understand style.

GPU Newsletter: distributed every month to all managers and staff throughout the group. It focusses on personnel news and includes central and departmental initiatives, reports and surveys, covering a particular part of the group or the whole group. A recent survey showed that 75% of staff read *Newsletter* and a large number use it as their major source of personnel information.

GPU News-in-Brief: introduced in 1986 to supplement *GPU Newsletter;* appearing at least alternate months and going to all staff in the group. It gives early information about topics likely to affect all or most staff. Some of these will then be covered in formal circulars, but in other cases the *News-in-Brief* coverage will do away with the need for a circular.

Total editorial, production, and distribution costs for these two newsletters come to around £20,000 a year.

annual reports

Most major — and many smaller — government departments produce annual reports; in some cases there are statutory requirements to report on specific activities. Departments like Her Majesty's Stationery Office (HMSO) and Crown Suppliers, which are run as 'trading funds', produce colourful illustrated reports much like those produced by companies in the private sector.

Large private sector employers also often produce special versions for staff of their annual report and accounts, setting out financial information in clear, graphic form. In some cases these employee reports are distributed as part of a company newspaper or magazine. Annual reports to staff are still rare in the Civil Service.

Example
Export Credits Guarantee Department (ECGD)

ECGD produced its first report to staff in 1983/84. It showed in graphic form the volume and value of business handled by the Department, summarised ECGD's financial position, and listed significant developments during the year.

In 1986 the National Audit Office (NAO) recommended that *all* departments should produce annual reports, including information about their aims, objectives and achieved performance. The NAO also commended the efforts being made to improve the presentation of Government reports, including the use of graphics, different typefaces and colour.

A few points to bear in mind
(adapted from Appendix B to *Employee Involvement*, Peat, Marwick, Mitchell & Co. 1983 — see page 62):

- show the importance senior management attaches to the employee report: include a statement by the head of the organisation;
- use the report as a medium to encourage employees to feel proud of the organisation;
- include a few names and photographs of employees;
- write in clear and unambiguous language; use illustrations — but don't be patronising.

personnel and line management documents

Over the last few years increasing emphasis has been put on the role of line managers in the Civil Service and their prime responsibility for personnel matters. There have been a number of service-wide initiatives in personnel management and increased delegation of responsibility to line managers. Many departments have had to take a close look at their existing practices, make sure that line managers are fully aware of developments, and issue new guidelines.

Departments have also realised that it is important to involve the people who have to make use of written instructions whenever they are being revised. Several departments, including Inland Revenue, and HM Customs and Excise, have carried out formal surveys of internal working instructions to check that they are 'user friendly'. It is also important to look at the *distribution* of operating instructions and similar paper: it is easy to swamp staff in local offices with daily masses of paper. Inland Revenue, as part of the follow-up to its communications survey (see page 21) experimented with a system of bunching different kinds of working and general management notices together every two weeks — the *Fortnightly Information Bundle (FIB)* system. Ministry of Agriculture, Fisheries and Food (MAFF) has a system for preparing instructions to staff carrying out the many statutory duties in its regional and area offices which makes sure that headquarters and regional divisions work together on new instructions.

Example
Her Majesty's Land Registry — Accountable Management
In recent years district registries within the Land Registry have operated management systems similar in principle but differing in their scope and coverage. These differences gave rise to uncertainty as to the Department's 'policy'. A working party reviewed existing procedures in order to bring together the best features of existing practice and introduce simple and consistent documentation and procedures throughout the Department.

As a result a new booklet, *Accountable Management in the Land Registry*, was prepared, discussed with the departmental trade unions, and issued to all those who were currently, or likely to be, responsible for staff. The system centres on the creation of a 'Manager's Guide' and requires periodic performance reviews for all managers and most of their staff. The book explains the policy, practice and procedures. The individual manager's role within the organisation is clarified and constructive communication made easier at all levels. All managers were asked to prepare a guide in the new format in consultation with their immediate line managers and to establish a time-table for periodic reviews.

Example
**Lord Chancellor's Department —
Personnel Management Policy
Statement**

All government departments have been
drawing up and issuing personnel
management policy statements. Timing,
style and format have varied considerably.
The Lord Chancellor's Department did the
work in three stages:
(i)   advance information sheets announced
      the advent and intention of the
      statement;
(ii) the statement itself confirmed and
      detailed both policy and practice in all
      areas of personnel-related activities;
(iii) leaflets translated the statement into a
      readable form for all staff.

The stages cost respectively:
(i)   £130
(ii) £500
(iii) £8,000
Effectiveness of the publications is being
monitored through existing departmental
machinery and exchanges between
personnel officers in meetings and
correspondence.

points to remember

1. **Objectives** Departments need to be clear
about the objectives of any written publications
they introduce. These may include:
- fostering a sense of community/corporate
  identity;
- transmitting management information to
  staff;
- transmitting 'specialist' technical up-to-
  date information to relevant groups;
- giving staff an opportunity to comment
  on and question management policies and
  practices;
- focusing attention on certain aspects of
  the manager's job.

2. **Target readership** Different types of
publications may be needed depending on their
aim: all staff or specific groups.

3. **Format and style** Different formats will be appropriate to the various types of publications, depending on their objectives.

4. **Costs** The overall budget for each publication needs to be identified first since this will affect format, style and production methods. In the case of house journals, consider the use of income from advertising space.

5. **Production methods** In-house/external resources need to be costed and compared.

6. **News gathering** A reliable and regular source of contributors is needed.

7. **Editorial policy** Needs to be settled at the outset. Close relations between the editor and senior management are needed in order to secure accurate, up-to-date information. A degree of editorial independence is usually needed if a balanced view of events is to be given and publications are not to be seen simply as management propaganda.

8. **Feedback/evaluation** Communications are a two-way process. It is important that staff news and comments on publications are encouraged and made known. While this gives an indication of the value of the publication, an attitude survey is probably necessary for an accurate assessment.

9. **Involvement** Best of all, involve the people who will make use of the written material throughout its preparation.

10. **Plain English** Stick to short sentences, everyday words. Try draft notices or instructions on test panels of typical readers.

4. improving oral communications

'Bosses, colleagues and subordinates need to be kept sufficiently informed. This can be well managed only by talking to people in a manner they respect.'

Andrew Kakabadse, *Professor of Management Development, Cranfield School of Management (Sunday Times, 27 April 1986).*

Oral communications are vital in any organisation if work is to be carried out efficiently, and if people are to feel happy in their work and know where and how they fit into the scheme of things. Many civil servants spend a great deal of time talking to people over local office counters, explaining complicated rules and regulations, or briefing busy ministers. Much inter- and intra- departmental work is done in meetings and on the telephone. Despite this, pressure of work often means that managers say they find it difficult to find time to talk to their own staff, keeping them in touch with developments, and explaining the reasons for changes in practices and procedures.

cascade/team briefing

A number of departments have introduced or experimented with Cascade and Team Briefing systems.

Cascade Briefing systems are essentially techniques to ensure the effective passing of information up and down the management chain. Their primary direction is downwards but good practice should also encourage upward messages. Meetings are held regularly and involve only a few people to encourage the exchange of views. Team Briefing, a system pioneered by the Industrial Society, is a systematic and structured 'cascading' procedure.

Cascade systems are arguably of most use in organisations where the ratio of staff in higher and lower grades is relatively small and where the hierarchy is not so long that messages become distorted.

Example
Export Credits Guarantee Department (ECGD) — monthly line briefings

Following a communications survey, ECGD introduced monthly line briefings to bring information about developments, instructions and notices to the attention of all staff.

The meetings themselves last for no more than half an hour but often form part of other regular meetings line managers have with their staff. They start at Grade 5 level and then cascade down through the grade hierarchy. Each officer conducting a briefing provides the participants with a written brief summarising the points covered. Subjects are covered in different ways at the various levels, depending on the needs of the individual.

Other departments which have introduced Team Briefing or other cascade systems include: Her Majesty's Stationery Office, DHSS, Department of National Savings, Property Services Agency, HM Treasury.

Quality Circles

A Quality Circle is a group of between five and 12 people, preferably from the same work area, who meet regularly to analyse problems that affect them.

Having agreed on which problems to tackle, they work together to find solutions, using a variety of problem-solving techniques in which the circle leader, or facilitator, can be trained.

The circle makes formal presentations to management of their findings, solutions and action plan. Not only does this make sure action is taken on specific problems, it also helps improve general communication within the organisation, and develop personal skills of members of the circle. In the private sector a number of successful companies have adapted Circles to suit their needs, as one element of a total quality approach to their operation.

Example
Department of Trade and Industry (DTI)

In 1983 three quality circles were formed within two headquarters divisions of DTI. Line management made time available for initial training and for regular meetings — about one hour per week for each circle. Staff involved — on an entirely voluntary basis — were all at SEO level or below, the majority at EO level or below.

One circle concentrated, initially, on problems affecting the management of paper within the division; one looked at catering for staff and problems associated with internal meetings and the third in a licensing section of Radio-communications Division examined a problem of delays in receiving licensing fee receipts. In all cases presentations were made to senior management, and action taken.

Additional benefits perceived by staff taking part included:

- quick identification of a wide range of common problems — over 40 in one group;
- personal development of members of the teams; appreciation of the need for self-discipline;
- opportunity to meet colleagues from other parts of the division;
- chance to improve communications with senior management;
- boost to staff morale and confidence;
- concentrating attention on particular problems.

A useful by-product from DTI's point of view is that the experiment — which could be copied in other parts of the Department — can be used as an example when talking about ways to involve staff in improving quality, when encouraging other employers to take part in the National Quality Campaign.

'It is really rewarding to work with colleagues to find solutions to problems. It develops minds, it develops people; it adds to the scope of our jobs and to job satisfaction'.

DTI quality circle member

working with trades unions

There is, of course, continual consultation with the Civil Service trades unions about pay and conditions of service of civil servants. The National Whitley system provides a framework at national, departmental and local levels. But in addition a number of departments have set up specific initiatives with the trades unions; one of them is summarised below. Other departments who have set up joint programmes with trades unions include Export Credits Guarantee Department and Ordnance Survey.

getting policy makers and case workers together

'A listening leadership is essential because each person in a business has at least one good idea on how to achieve the task better.'

John Adair, visitng Professor in Leadership Studies, University of Sussex *(Sunday Times* 18 May 1986).

There can be many divides in departments — geographical, hierarchical — which hinder efficient working. Policy workers and headquarters staff sometimes operate in isolation from case workers and staff in the regions, yet, in order to be able to do their own work well, it is essential for them to understand the needs of the others. A number of departments have been doing a great deal to help bring such staff closer together. One example is the linked offices arrangements within the DHSS (see below). Others include the working parties also operated by the DHSS where headquarters and regional and local staff are brought together on a regular basis; or management/staff seminars such as those held by the Immigration and Nationality Department of the Home Office, where EO/HEO case workers and policy makers are brought together. The Northern Region of the Unemployment Benefit Service in the Department of Employment Group runs regular 'Team Building' meetings, which bring together local and regional management teams to exchange problems and ideas in a residential setting.

Less conventional methods include summer schools for EOs run by DHSS, and regular EO-level conferences held by MAFF. DHSS have also introduced a series of 'road shows' or presentations and discussions led by teams of personnel officers from Headquarters, aimed at informing staff of major changes in personnel practices and the introduction of new management skills.

Example
Department of Health and Social Security — linked offices

In DHSS, individual sections in the Social Security Operations Division at Headquarters are each linked with a small number of local offices. This enables them to get quick feedback from the field on operations and policy developments, either before or after the event; and enables the linked offices to get involved in the development of change that will affect them and the way they do their work. Linked offices are asked to comment on the application of policy, procedures and instructions from the local office point of view. In this way a view from the 'sharp end' can be brought to bear, and particular problems, perhaps not perceived by policy makers or operations staff at the centre, can be revealed and if possible put right. Linked offices are also used as informal sounding boards on new ideas and developments. From a relatively modest beginning in 1983, the network of linked offices had grown by 1986 to over 100.

A review showed that linking is a popular initiative:

- HQ sections find their linked offices to be rich quarries of operational expertise;
- there is scope to develop relationships, despite problems of time and travel costs that tell against linked offices in provincial locations;
- linked offices are pleased to be given the opportunity to make a contribution to the development of change.

training in communication skills

Poor presentational skills can quickly sabotage any oral communications system. Departments have recognised that managers in any organisation need help and training in oral briefing. Management training at the Civil Service College and within departments treats good communications as an integral part of good management.

Example
Civil Service College — line briefing

In 1986 the Civil Service College introduced a new line-briefing training service. Based on a half-day session, either on site or at the College, the seminar goes beyond simple techniques of effective presentation to deal, for example, with problems experienced in addressing one's own staff and dealing positively with their questions and concerns.

Departments who want to extend the training to individual coaching, using closed circuit TV, can do so with a Training Design Pack provided by the College.

Many other departments have introduced training courses or modules on effective presentation, on Team Briefing, and on 'influencing skills'. They include: Department of Employment; DHSS; ECGD.

points to remember

1. Planning To be effective, oral communications need to be well planned and structured. A formal framework, such as a Cascade Briefing system, ensures that time will be made available. Care must be taken to avoid messages becoming distorted.

2. Back-up Oral communications need to be backed up by the written word to ensure that the right message gets across.

3. Selection and training Although some of the skills of effective presentation can be taught, good oral communicators should be identified and used to pass information to staff.

4. Feedback Oral communication is a two-way process: meetings should be discussions rather than monologues.

5. Short-circuits Avoid the danger of cascade systems becoming too rigid and hierarchical: get senior managers to 'grade skip' downwards and meet junior staff regularly.

5. using video

Video can personalise communications. It enables busy managers to talk to more people than they could otherwise reach and it helps put across messages in an interesting way. Consistent messages can be transmitted quickly. While fully polished videos can take several weeks to produce, it is possible to produce urgent messages on a simple scale within a week. As one-off exercises these short videos have little effect; as part of regular management/staff communications they can be useful. Video needs to be a part of a communications strategy, not used in isolation: proper supporting material and an opportunity for discussion are essential. It should not be used as a method of avoiding personal contact. Video has weaknesses: it is not suitable for transmitting lengthy or detailed information; it does not ensure all questions are answered promptly; it does not replace other media such as house journals and news bulletins: but it can do things they cannot. Video has been widely used in the Civil Service in the past mainly for training purposes, but departments are now experimenting with other uses.

Example
Department of Health and Social Security (DHSS)

DHSS has made several experiments in the use of video for management communications as well as for training. Its in-house production unit has been producing programmes at the rate of over 20 a year on a wide range of topics from staff welfare to new technology.

Local offices have some 27 titles at their disposal including:

- **'Ready, willing and able?'** — a programme which helps staff recognise the less obvious signs of physical and mental disability in people calling for help and advice at local offices. It illustrates ways of dealing with disabled callers so as to make the most effective use of their visit and help them retain their dignity.
- **'A word in your ear'** — a programme aimed at making effective and economic use of the telephone through conversation techniques.
- **'Staff budgeting'** — this programme helped to introduce a new and flexible way of matching staffing to workload in a local office, giving managers more accountability and control.

The local office video experiment was evaluated in the summer of 1986 and there was overwhelming support for the use of videos from managers and staff, local office trainers, and trainees.

Other departments which have used video for management communications include: Department of Trade and Industry; Inland Revenue.

points to remember

1. Video in isolation is ineffective: use it as part of a communications strategy.
2. Think what are the real aims of the video: don't be seduced by the medium.
3. Provide written briefing and follow-up material.

4. Use video for short, straightforward messages: complex videos are expensive and may confuse the audience.
5. Make sure you get feedback.
6. Don't be afraid to try out ideas first: eg on a test panel of viewers representing the wider audience.

6. rewarding staff suggestions and inventions

Most government departments have long-established schemes that reward staff who suggest improvements to working practices.

There is also provision for giving suitable awards to inventors, where there is either a use for the invention within the public sector or the prospect of income from commercial exploitation.

Managers who have responsibility for staff suggestions schemes meet periodically to exchange information. A general review of guidelines and procedures in 1986 gave a fresh impetus to departments looking at the organisation of their schemes, the scale of rewards and the publicity given to them.

Example
Department of Health and Social Security (DHSS)

DHSS runs a particularly lively staff suggestions scheme. Staff are actively encouraged to contribute their ideas and there is a computer-aided system for helping speedy consideration of suggestions. The benefits to the Civil Service have often been significant, justifying substantial awards. In recent years senior management and ministers in the Department have shown their interest by taking part in an annual award-giving ceremony, held in London, for the most successful contributors. Publicity has been given to this event in departmental newspapers.

In the year ending 5 April, 1987, some 6,691 suggestions were received and 520 ideas accepted, with estimated savings of

£0.75 million. Awards given amounted to
over £70,000; administration costs were
around £195,000 a year.

points to remember

Any award scheme must have the overall aim of
encouraging suggestions, ideas and inventions
that make or save money for the organisation,
through their effective implementation or
exploitation.
Plus:
1. Suggestions need to be dealt with quickly
   and flexibly.
2. Rules must be accessible to all staff and easy
   to understand.
3. Keep size of awards as flexible as possible.
4. Get maximum publicity, internal or external.
5. Watch out for Intellectual Property Rights
   etc.
6. Keep the scheme under constant review: do
   not let it become ossified.

7. group incentive schemes

Group incentive schemes can help promote
effective team-work and greater efficiency by
suitably recognising the efforts of successful
groups. In government departments, local
managements have been given discretion to
'plough back' some of the resultant efficiency
savings to reward such groups.

Rewards can take the form of improved
amenities or improvements to the office
environment, cash, or voucher payments. The
schemes should complement the Financial
Management Initiative (FMI): such projects were
advocated by the Government in its White Paper
Efficiency and effectiveness in the Civil Service,
Cmnd 8616. HMSO, 1982.

Group incentive schemes are probably most
suitable where a number of units are engaged
on similar work, such as a local office network,
and where the collective effort of work groups is
essential to high achievement of tasks. Schemes
should be easier to devise where clear measures
of performance are readily obtainable, as in case
work or processing areas. Assessments of
performance should normally be made against
pre-determined yardsticks; on a historic basis in

relation to past achievements; and by comparison between offices or units. Pilot schemes in some departments have provided lessons for future experiments.

Example
Department of Health and Social Security (DHSS)

DHSS conducted a two-year exercise involving three different elements:

- Group Managers, using their own criteria, made awards for good or improved overall performance to the top two-thirds of offices in their commands;
- Regional Controllers awarded £500 to the office with the most praiseworthy performance in the region, and £250 each to the two who had made most improvements in the standard of service to the public;
- Offices kept 25% of any administrative savings, up to a maximum of £1,000, which arose from suggestions from groups of staff for improving efficiency (to which they were not already committed).

Managers of offices receiving awards were given discretion to spend the money, other than for political purposes, for the benefit of all their staff, in providing, for example, better office or recreational facilities or boosting the sports and social club funds.

---

8. job satisfaction

'No matter how good pay and conditions may be, they cannot adequately compensate for work that is monotonous and lacking in challenge.'

Christine Howarth, *The Way People Work.*

The carrying out of monotonous tasks under pressure by bored, frustrated staff, who do not understand how the job they do fits into the broader picture, leads to low productivity, lack of motivation, and poor morale. Greater job satisfaction and better productivity are not brought about easily. A change in management style is sometimes needed. But management cannot act in isolation: the best expertise to deal with many problems in a department already exists within the organisation itself.

Many of the initiatives within departments have been helped by the work of the Job Satisfaction Team from the Cabinet Office (OMCS). The Team works in government departments and agencies alongside their own staff. The Team's job is to help people help themselves. It seeks to find ways of using all the talents within an organisation, helping staff to analyse their main problems, to find solutions, and to put those solutions into practice. The approach aims at continuing development rather than a one-off exercise. Everyone concerned in the area of work has the opportunity to be involved and have a say in any proposed changes. To ensure proper liaison with the normal Civil Service Whitley machinery, the work is jointly steered by official and trades union sides at all levels from national to local.

Example
National Health Service Central Register (NHSCR)

The NHSCR is the central record of all NHS patients for England and Wales. It is used mainly by Family Practitioner Committees in connection with Patient Registration with general practitioners. Located in Southport, it employs about 600 people. In 1982 both management and trades unions were looking for ways of preparing people in a labour intensive operation, where things had been done in much the same way for many years, for big organisational changes including computerisation. It was decided to involve the Job Satisfaction Team (JST) to help with this work.

Between October 1982 and January 1983 the combined NHSCR/JST interviewed individually almost 200 people from all grades — about one-third of the office staff. Staff raised some 70 issues on work procedure, training, personnel management, mangement style etc.

Clerical staff began tackling some of these issues; others were considered during seminars held for different levels of management. After about a year an appreciable change in atmosphere had taken place: there was now a general awareness of the need for improved communications. It was then decided to bring together all of the activity and tackle some of the fundamental issues.

One important development was the setting up of experimental 'whole job' clerical teams led by Executive Officers (EOs) as an alternative to the existing production-line method. Eventually 'whole job' working was adopted throughout the office. Other activity included:

- a multi-grade working party recommended a more customer-oriented alternative to the existing organisation structure; this has now become the 'norm' across the whole office. There is scarcely a unit in the organisation that does not now have a clearly defined customer base (mostly external), for whom it is providing a service and with whom it has established a direct relationship;
- in one area of work, staff contributed to the introduction of VDUs;
- a clerical group put together job training guidelines, and all new entrants are now attached initially to a 'basic skills' training unit where they are given intensive introductory job training across all Central Register activites;
- a group of Higher Executive Officers (HEOs) devised and put into operation a new and more equitable policy for staff movements.

By September 1985, 'ownership' of all this activity was taken over by NHSCR staff from the JST. The NHSCR staff who had been steering the activities became an Employee Participation Group; they issued to all staff an office statement of policy on employee participation. This multi-grade group chaired by the Senior Manager with TUS and representatives from all parts of the Office, meets regularly to discuss and make recommendations on matters of interest concerned with work: procedures, accommodation, environmental issues (such as car parking and smoking in the workplace) and any other topics which might be raised by those attending. An office newsletter is being developed.

Benefits

Apart from the successful introduction of 'whole job' working, relationships between management and staff improved; long-established barriers were broken down; and there was increased participation at all levels in decision making.

The reorganisation of the office not only created an effective customer-oriented operation, but also one better prepared to tackle forthcoming computerisation.

Despite the considerable changes and a 10% increase in workload since the project began, plus a higher proportion of documents needing more complicated processing, productivity levels nearly 20% higher were being achieved by early 1986.

In an office where the work pattern had hardly changed in 40 years, a massive reorganisation of operating practice was achieved with the full co-operation of staff and trades unions. A better service was provided to customers and, through that, more pride in the job and job satisfaction.

Other departments where employee involvement has been enhanced by the job satisfaction approach include: HM Customs and Excise; Inland Revenue; Lord Chancellor's Department; Driver and Vehicle Licensing Centre. Two of the projects are illustrated in the video *Thinking People* (see page 70).

9. involving staff in introduction of new technology

'New technology gives you two choices: creating monotonous, repetitive jobs dealing with only one part of a process or creating varied, more rewarding jobs. Most boring jobs are created by default rather than design.'

The Winning Streak Workout Book. **Goldsmith and Clutterbuck.**

Like other organisations, government departments have been gradually introducing new technology to their operations. Computers, word processors, and other IT equipment are now as much a part of the working environment as the desk and the filing cabinet. Information technology is being applied pervasively to all aspects of the day-to-day work of civil servants.

Changing to IT makes it imperative to know more about all aspects of the jobs that people do: the everyday problems they have in dealing with the public or with other departments. The mechanistic approach of traditional systems analysis tended to miss the more personal dimensions of people's jobs: what they learn from experience. The complications that can arise from gaps in understanding like this can make or break new computer systems when they become operational.

Introducing new technology means involving the experts — those who do the jobs everyday — so that the right system can be designed to match what people are trying to do and what they need to do the job.

Management guidelines (see page 68) produced for the Civil Service by Cabinet Office (MPO) on introducing office technology emphasise that managers, operators and direct users of new equipment should be involved in the planning and design of office technology systems as well as their implementation. All this is easier said than done. The Central Computer and Telecommunications Agency (CCTA) of HM Treasury plans a handbook on IT design and implementation. It will be designed to help users develop and clarify what they need to think about in contributing effectively to the design and implementations of their own systems. The handbook itself is an example of user involvement: CCTA are trying out ideas for it on representatives from a number of departments as the book takes shape. An important feedback from this test panel is that users of the technology need to drive their own IT projects — not just contribute to or comment upon someone else's ideas.

'How to stifle innovation: *A selection of ways in which organisations commonly make introduction of new ideas difficult...*

- *Regard any new idea from below with suspicion.*
- *Insist that people who need your approval first go through several other levels of management.*
- *Get divisions and individuals to challenge each other's proposals.*
- *Criticise freely, withhold praise.*
- *Treat identification of problems as a sign of failure.*
- *Control everything carefully and count everything in sight frequently.*
- *Make decisions in secret and spring them on people.*
- *Do not hand out information freely.*
- *Get lower managers to implement your threatening decisions.*
- *Never forget that senior management already know everything important about the business.'*

Rosabeth Moss Kanter *The Change Masters.*

Example
Driver and Vehicle Licensing Centre (DVLC)

Staff at DVLC had become increasingly involved in system planning, first in overcoming problems associated with the introduction of large computer systems, then pioneering the concept of job satisfaction (see page 51) in the Civil Service. When the time came to replace the ageing computers, there was a readiness to re-design the whole system and not simply replace the computers.

The new computers at DVLC not only carry out updating of the main file in batch mode as before, but also drive 1,500 VDUs for input of transactions and for making on-line enquiries. This additional service affects the work of 2,500 clerical staff and 500 data processors.

Staff involvement
Staff loaned full time from the clerical areas, working alongside systems analysts, prepared a comprehensive 'user

requirement'. It covered not only the system requirements concerning input, screen design, processing and output, but also matters of equal importance to the clerical users: environmental and ergonomic issues associated with VDUs; changes in microfilm procedures; training (both on the VDU and managing change); and the effects of integrating clerical and data processing staff.

The next objective was to ensure as much involvement as possible by the staff themselves in planning the new system. Staff were asked to try out part of the new system — eg prototype VDUs — and validate new training methods. All large branches held regular consultative meetings representing all grades to discuss progress throughout.

All staff, whether involved in trials or not, were given two video-based presentations at which they discussed the project and proposals. Their comments, together with feedback from EOs and above who attended 'Management of change' courses, were considered by system designers. This close co-operation by users and analysts led to more flexibility and greater understanding of each other's problems.

User tests
The final objective was to allow users to test the completed system. After procurement, user acceptance trials were followed by a full-scale pilot trial using live work and lasting a year. By the end of the year, 200 staff were involved in the trial and they had been able to try out many variations of workflow around their VDU allocation. Progress was monitored by the staff themselves and reported to their colleagues in a series of branch house magazines.

Written reports on the user requirement, the pilot trials plan, and the pilot trial report were discussed and agreed by management boards, chaired by users and with the trades unions in a joint working party.

Benefits outweigh costs
The benefits of closer involvement by users outweigh the costs of around £240,000 pa. Over two years of the implementation phase of the project, those costs have to be viewed in relation to DVLC running costs (currently £106 million pa) and the total cost of replacement computer projects (£35 million).

Another department with extensive experience of involving staff in the introduction of new technology is Her Majesty's Stationery Office.

IV useful publications and other sources

Assertiveness at Work
David Stubbs, Pan Business Books, 1986.

A do-it-yourself manual on self-improvement, written without jargon but with clear descriptions of varying forms of behaviour and simple suggestions on how behaviour can be modified so as to elicit favourable responses. There is a useful chapter on listening skills with many examples, some taken from the Civil Service. Study of this book cannot be a substitute for a good management training course, but it has sound advice and instances of how to use skills assertively.

British Employee Involvement Today: the practice and experience of CBI member companies
CBI, 1983.

A booklet summarising replies that the CBI got to a questionnaire, asking member companies about their employee involvement systems and practices.

Case Studies in Organisational Behaviour
Edited by Chris Clegg, Nigel Kemp and Karen Legge. Harper and Row, 1985.

There are 27 cases, all derived from empirical research and organised in three sections covering organisational behaviour, personnel management and industrial relations. The case studies are short enough to be useful (average 6–8pp), but include enough information to give some 'feel' of the problem and its context.

The Change Masters: corporate entrepreneurs at work
Rosabeth Moss Kantor, Allen and Unwin, 1984.

An examination of the pathways and pitfalls in the search for innovation at ten US companies, including Wang, Hewlett-Packard, General Motors. Among the factors making for 'corporate renaissance' in organisations, the author identifies: participative mechanisms, encouraging a cultural pride, improvement in lateral communications, access to top level support, fewer unnecessary layers in the hierarchy.

Communication at Work: a self-help guide for managers
Industrial Relations Services, 1986.

A guide for individual managers or supervisors concerned about communication with their own staff, colleagues and senior managers. Written in friendly question-and-answer style, the booklet has chapters on both the theory and practice of communication, not forgetting the need to measure effectiveness. Time and other resources needed to communicate information effectively should be balanced, say the authors, against benefits in productivity, industrial relations and morale. 'One thing is for sure: evidence from organisations throughout the world demonstrates conclusively that successful performance and good communication go hand in hand, although it is just as likely that success leads to good communication as vice versa.'

Democracy at Work
Tom Schuller, Oxford, OPUS, 1985.

The book traces changes in the features of working society and considers whether democratisation is a smooth evolutionary process or a cyclical pattern leading nowhere. Other topics include an examination of outstanding questions raised by the Bullock proposals concerning worker-directors. Tom Schuller's book contains a well constructed argument for greater democratisation of the workplace.

Employee Communications in British Industry
Vista Communications (15a George Street, Croydon, CRO 1LB), 1987.

Vista, a management consultancy specialising in communications, carried out a survey of British firms: one objective was to assess the impact of section 1 of the Employment Act 1982. The response was naturally biased towards companies already active in the field of employee communications. As a follow-up, Vista has now carried out a second annual survey of communications and copies of this are available from them.

Employee Communications in the Public Sector
Edited Geoff Perkins, Institute of Personnel Management, 1986.

Based on practical experience, mainly of IPM members in the public sector, this is a useful short handbook. It draws out problems that bedevil effective communications within large organisations. Individual chapters look at *why* communication is necessary, *what* and *how* to communicate, *who* should communicate, and to *whom*. Among other techniques, the book examines briefing groups and covers consultative arrangements and the interest of public sector trades unions. There are a number of case studies.

Employee Involvement: after the Employment Act 1982
Peat, Marwick, Mitchell, & Co., 1983.

Describes reporting requirements under the Employment Act 1982 and discusses some of the issues which may need to be addressed by companies reviewing their position on employee involvement.

Employee Involvement and Participation: principles and standards of practice — the IPA/IPM Code, 1983

Sets out both principles and standards of practice, and a suggested action guide for organisations.

Copies available from:
Industrial Participation Association, 85 Tooley Street, London SE1 2QZ; or Institute of Personnel Management, IPM House, Camp Road, London SW19 4UW.

The False Promise of the Japanese Miracle
S. Praakash Sethi, Nobuaki Namiki and Carl L. Swanson, Pitman, 1984.

Recommended to those who really wish to analyse the Japanese system of management and to see what can be translated to their own situation.

In Search of Excellence: lessons from America's best run companies
Thomas J. Peters and Robert H. Waterman Jr., Harper and Row, 1982.

Now a classic management text, this book centres on prescriptive characteristics of excellent organisations: a bias for action: staying close to the customer; autonomy and entrepreneurship; productivity through people; hands-on value driven; 'stick to the knitting' (avoid diversification); simple form, lean staff (or 'keep it simple stupid'); 'loose-tight' properties (balance centralised and decentralised).

Japanese Manufacturing Techniques: nine hidden lessons in simplicity
R.J. Schonberger, Free Press, 1982.

Gives a useful rundown on the Japanese approach to quality and to 'just in time' manufacture. Highly recommended for managers.

Leaders: the strategies for taking charge
Warren Bennis and Burt Nanus, Harper and Row, 1985.

From analysis of 90 'top leaders' in US business, politics, and public life, the authors distil the essence of 'transformative leadership': the ability to achieve significant change in an organisation, reflecting the community of interest of everyone in that organisation. The book includes a short and readable chapter on 'Managing through communication'.

Motivation and Job Design: theory, research, and practice
Ivan. T. Robertson and Mike Smith, Institute of Personnel Management, 1985.

A helpful primer on theories about motivation and job design, to be dipped into as a source of reference or an *aide memoire*. Sections on the use of questionnaires in measuring motivation and possible changes to job and work design to improve motivation cover the ground well.

The New Agenda
Francis Kinsman, Spencer Stuart Management Consultants, 1983.

The source material is the author's series of 30 interviews with leading businessmen and commentators, which revolved round the elaboration of answers to a single question: 'what do you imagine will be the most important

issues facing British management by 1990?'
Although there is a variety of views expressed,
the overall message is 'we shall have to do
things differently in future'. The last chapter sets
out the 'new agenda' under 32 headings.

Organisation: a guide to problems and practice
John Child, Harper and Row, 1984.

The focus of the book is on the structure of
work organisation in institutions. John Child
covers job design, the shape of work
organisation, its integration and control, and the
reward policies that are seen as complementary
to the process of control. Later chapters also
cover the impact of new technology, changing
the shape of organisation, systems and
procedures, and the relationship between these
and performance.

Passion for Excellence
Tom Peters and Nancy Austin, Random House,
1985.

The authors call for a rapid return to basics —
pride in one's organisation and enthusiasm for
its work. They focus on clearing up bureaucratic
junk — 'overstaffed middle management and
layers of staff get in the way'. If a manager
concentrates on the people in the unit, superior
service and constant innovation will follow.

Sections on 'Management by wandering around
(or walking about)' and 'Service to the
customer' provide common sense insights,
helpful check lists, and practical examples.

Reality of Management
Rosemary Stewart, Pan, 1967.

The author's first and perhaps best known book,
built upon findings of her extensive diary studies
of what managers do in their jobs. It represented
something of a landmark in thinking about
management education. The book contains a lot
of advice on how to plan for change, make the
right decision, define objectives and
communicate effectively, based on hard data
from diaries and interviews.

Skills for Effective Communication: a guide to building relationships
R.J. Becvar, Wiley, 1974.

A useful book of exercises and activities to be carried out in pairs. The exercises, which are preceded by sections on related theory, cover skills of attention, understanding verbal messages, expressing feelings, conflict resolution, feedback, and negotiation. For each skill, a chart is provided for plotting your progress.

Successful Suggestion Schemes
The Industrial Society, 1986.

New edition of a useful pocket book, which combines general guidance on setting up a suggestions scheme with the report of a survey carried out by the Industrial Society among 350 different organisations. The authors conclude that the five factors essential to a successful scheme are: management support; forward-looking human relations policy; good communications policy; efficient and fair administration; adequate publicity.

The Superteam Solution: successful teamworking in organisations
C. Hastings, P. Bixby and R. Chaudry-Lawton, Gower, 1986.

Superteams are different: they are quick sorties into the fog, getting control of the twin engines of success and inbuilt tendency to self-destruct! 'For them working is fun and fun is work...They don't ever use the word failure'. If you are ever fortunate enough to find such people in your organisation, who is going to lead them? The book provides the answer. It is written in an easily understood, explicit style, and it challenges many of our underlying values and assumptions.

The Way People Work: job satisfaction and the challenge of change
Christine Howarth, Oxford University Press, 1984.

Christine Howarth was for ten years an adviser to the Civil Service Job Satisfaction Team. After an initial analysis of where and why things go wrong in organisations and how they can be put right, the book concentrates on case studies, including the Civil Service itself.

White Collar Quality Circles: a study
Department of Management Sciences, J. Lees and Barrie Dale, Occasional Paper No. 8510, October 1985.

The first paper presents the finding of research carried out in August 1985. The evidence from the surveys was that white collar QCs are not significantly more difficult to initiate, but that there can be problems sustaining them.

The second paper sets out the findings of a questionnaire survey of 27 organisations in the service sector with QC programmes. In general the researchers found major new differences between the way in which circle programmes are implemented and operated in service and in manufacturing organisations. The report ends with comments reflecting on the apparent difficulty of sustaining QCs in some service sector organisations.

The Winning Streak: Britain's top companies reveal their strategies for success. W. Goldsmith and D. Clutterbuck, Weidenfeld and Nicholson, 1984.

The British version of *In Search of Excellence* (see above) and as such rather derivative in technique and content. The authors look at the attributes of successful British companies and blend them together in the same broad way as do Peters and Waterman. Best to dip into, for descriptions of, for example, Marks & Spencer's successful philosophies and management practice.

The Winning Streak Workout Book
W. Goldsmith and D. Clutterbuck, Weidenfeld and Nicholson, 1985.

Yet another sequel to a successful first book. The *Workout Book* is divided into sections on 'winning through: leadership; autonomy; control' etc. Each chapter has a questionnaire that fires awkward questions at managers, aiming to get them to think afresh about how well company and individual managers measure up against best practice. The chapter and questionnaire on 'Winning through involvement' are hard-hitting and well worth reading.

Advisory, Conciliation and Arbitration Service, Work Research Unit Publications

Effective and Satisfactory Work Systems: notes on some important features of their design and operation
G. White, 1983.

These notes, guidelines, and checklists are brought together from a number of sources. They concentrate on some of the organisational features of the process of industrial and commercial developments that are of sufficient size to warrant investment of time, effort and training in the process itself.

Forming the Future through Working Together
D. Cuthbert, A. Smith, and R. Sell, 1984.

Describes the participation project that is going on in Formica Ltd., in which the WRU has an advisory role.

Improving the Quality of Working Life (QWL) in the 1980s
Oliver Tynan, 1980.

This paper discusses the reasons why employers, trades unions and governments should work together for improvements in the quality of working life. It also comments on work that has been done to improve QWL.

New Office Technology: people, work structure and the process of change
L. Thompson, 1985.

Tracing the developments in office technology and the impact on information workers, this book is addressed particularly to managers, staff representatives and others who have responsibilities in this area. The main argument is that the rapid pace of technological developments has created many pressures on businesses, and the human aspects of technological change are in danger of being neglected.

The Work Research Unit, ACAS, produces a bi-monthly abstract bulletin designed to inform you about recent books, articles and reports. To

receive it on a regular basis write to
The Librarian, Work Research Unit, St. Vincent
House, 30 Orange Street, London WC2H 7HH
who will add your name to its mailing list. For
general enquiries about WRU publications,
phone 01-839 9289.

Civil Service publications

Assessment of Team Briefing at Chessington Computer Centre
Cabinet Office (MPO), 1984.

An account of the experimental introduction of
Team Briefing to the 400 staff at this centre,
which is responsible for pay of civil servants in a
number of government departments. Copies
available from PM2 Division, Cabinet Office
(OMCS), Room 69G, Government Offices,
Horse Guards Road, London SW1P 3AL.

Guide for New Managers
Cabinet Office (MPO) (formerly Civil Service
Department), HMSO, 1979.

This remains a good primer not only for civil
servants but for other new managers. It is just
as useful as a refresher for managers who have
been in post for some time. The central chapter,
'Working with People', emphasises the need for
teamwork and the manager's responsibility to
ensure good communications between the
members of the team. Currently being revised.

Improving Communications and Employee Involvement in the Civil Service: reports on seminars held 1985–1987

A series bringing together senior managers in
departments who have responsibility for internal
communications in government departments.
The present book stems, in part at least, from
discussion at these seminars. Copies available
from PM2 Division, Cabinet Office (OMCS),
Room 69G, Government Offices, Horse Guards
Road, London SW1P 3AL.

Introducing Office Technology: guidelines for management practice

One of a series of short management guidelines,
addressed to staff responsible for introducing

and managing office technology systems. Copies available from: HM Treasury/Cabinet Office Library, Great George Street, London SW1P 3AL.

Personnel Policies and the Management of Change: the report of a one-day seminar held by the Civil Service College and Peat, Marwick on 9 July 1985. Peat, Marwick, McClintock, reprinted 1987.

The theme of this seminar was 'managing change through personnel'. Four issues were examined: 'The role of the personnel function in managing change'; 'Monitoring and assessing personnel policy and practice'; 'Making the best use of people'; 'Relating personnel strategy to organisation objectives'.

Service to the Public: a handbook of good practice
DHSS, 1983/1987.

A compendium of ideas, all contributed by the staff of DHSS local offices, for improving service to the public. They include, for example, a number of ideas pioneered by individual offices for improving reception areas and accommodation in general; better ways of dealing with telephone calls; strengthening the links between local offices and the communities they serve; and liaison with other organisations. A revised edition of the handbook is scheduled for publication in late 1987.

Study of Management-Staff Communications in the Civil Service
Cabinet Office (MPO) and HM Treasury, 1985. 2 volumes.

The report on a study by Coopers & Lybrand Associates, involving 4,000 staff in six government departments. The consultants were asked to review the way in which information on subjects for which the two central departments are responsible is communicated to non-industrial civil servants. Such subjects include pay and conditions of service, personnel policies, and general management matters. A summary of the report is available from PM2 Division, Cabinet Office (OMCS), Room 69G, Government Offices, Horse Guards Road, London SW1P 3AL.

Job Satisfaction publications

The Civil Service Road to Job Satisfaction
Alan Hodgson, reprinted from *Personnel Management*, October 1985.

Job Satisfaction in the Civil Service
A folder containing updated case studies of projects where the Cabinet Office (OMCS) Job Satisfaction Team has worked with managers and staff in different government departments to improve the effectiveness of the organisation and the staff's own satisfaction with their work.

Participation, Teamwork and Practical Learning in the Civil Service
David Shaw, Work Research Unit Occasional Paper 33, January 1985.

All available from:
Job Satisfaction Team, Room 65a/G, Cabinet Office (OMCS), Horse Guards Road, London SW1P 3AL.

Video programmes

Quality of Working Life
This video was produced for the ACAS Work Research Unit. It shows how three major British companies — Eaton (Transmission Division), Formica, and May and Baker — worked jointly with trades unions and employees to develop participation programmes, quality circles, task forces, and similar innovations. Documentary footage from the companies is linked by a panel discussion.

Copies of the 25-minute video in VHS, Sony U-matic and Betamax formats can be bought or hired for preview from: CFL Vision, Chalfont Grove, Gerrards Cross, Bucks, SL9 8TN (tel. 02407 4433). Charge for 5-day hire (1986), £6.52 plus VAT.

Thinking People
A 33-minute video dealing with the effects of successful Job Satisfaction (JS) programmes within two government departments.

Thinking People is a documentary that takes a small but representative cross section of staff, managers and TU representatives and asks them to talk about what their work was like before the introduction of the JS programme. By documenting individual reactions, the video illustrates what can be achieved by the JS approach.

Copies of the video available for hire at £10 inc. VAT or purchase at £25 inc. VAT (£35 inc. VAT for U-matic version) from: CFL Vision, Chalfont Grove, Gerrards Cross, Bucks, SL9 8TN (tel. 02407 4433).

Ministry of Agriculture, Fisheries and Food

Manpower Division
Ministry of Agriculture, Fisheries and Food
Victory House
30–34 Kingsway
London WC2B 6TE

Tel: 01-405 4310 ext 587
GTN: 2556 587

Cabinet Office (Office of the Minister for the Civil Service)

Personnel Management Division 2
Room 69/G
Cabinet Office (OMCS)
Government Offices
Horse Guards Road
London SW1P 3AL

Tel: 01-270 6283
GTN: 270 6283

Job Satisfaction Team
Rm. 65a/b
Cabinet Office (OMCS)
Government Offices
Horse Guards Road
London SW1P 3AL

Tel: 01-270 6270
GTN: 270 6270

Central Computer – Telecommunications Agency

Riverwalk House
157–161 Millbank
London SW1P 4RT

Tel: 01-217 3298
GTN: 217 3298

Civil Service College

Directorate of Management Studies
Civil Service College
11 Belgrave Road
London SW1

Tel: 01-834 6644 ext 232
GTN: 2803 232

Crown Suppliers

See Property Services Agency

Ministry of Defence

Civilian Management (Industrial Relations)
Room 131
Northumberland House
Northumberland Avenue
London WC2N 5BP

Tel: 01-218 0974
GTN: 218 0974

Department of Employment Group

DE Group Personnel Unit
Room 723
Caxton House
Tothill Street
London SW1H 9NF

Tel: 01-213 5495
GTN: 213 5495

HM Customs and Excise

Departmental Communications Unit
Room 807
Dorset House
Stamford Street
London SE1 9PS

Tel: 01-928 0533 ext 2478/2505
GTN: 2523 2478/2505

Driver and Vehicle Licensing Centre

ADP, Room 16
DVLC
Longview Road
Swansea
S6 7AL

Tel: 0792 783013
GTN: 2413 3013

Department of the Environment/Transport

Room N13/19
2 Marsham Street
London SW1P 3EB

Tel: 01-212 4201
GTN: 212 4201

Exports Credits Guarantee Department

Personnel Management General Branch
Room 706
Export House
50 Ludgate Hill
London EC4M 7AY

Tel: 01-382 7038
GTN: 2890 7038

Department of Health and Social Security

Room A206
Department of Health and Social Security
Alexander Fleming House
Elephant and Castle
London SE1 6BY

Tel: 01-407 5522 ext 7227
GTN: 2915 7227

Home Office

Room 111
Home Office
Queen Anne's Gate
London SW1H 9AT

Tel: 01-213 4894
GTN: 213 4894

Prison Department

HM Prison HQ
Room 224
Cleland House
Page Street
London SW1P 4LN

Tel: 01-211 8936
GTN: 211 8936

Board of Inland Revenue

Inland Revenue
Management Division
Communications Group
New Wing
Somerset House
London WC2R 1LB

Tel: 01-438 7097
GTN: 2541 7097

Land Registry

HM Land Registry
Lincoln's Inn Fields
London WC2A 3PH

Tel: 01-405 3488 ext 394
GTN: 2504 394

Lord Chancellor's Department

Lord Chancellor's Department
Trevelyan House
Great Peter Street
London SW1P 2BY

Tel: 01-210 8660
GTN: 210 8660

Manpower Services Commission

Manpower Services Commission
Moorfoot
Sheffield S1 4PQ

Tel: 0742-703057
GTN: 2023 3057

National Audit Office

Room B441
Communication Unit
National Audit Office
157–197 Buckingham Palace Road
London SW1W 9SP

Tel: 01-798 7401
GTN: 2935 7401

Ordnance Survey

Head of Establishments
Ordnance Survey
Romsey Road
Maybush
Southampton SO9 4DH

Tel: 0703 792702
GTN: 2027 2702

Office of Population Censuses and Surveys

National Health Service Central Register
Smedley Hydro
Southport
Merseyside PR8 2HH

Tel: 0704 69824 ext 201

Property Services Agency — including the Crown Suppliers

PSA
Management Services Division
Lambeth Bridge House
London SE1 7SB

Tel: 01-211 0034
GTN: 211 0034

Public Record Office

Public Record Office
Kew
Richmond
Surrey TW9 4DU

Tel: 01-876 3444 ext 354

Scottish Office

Manpower and Organisation Division (Industrial Relations Branch)
Scottish Office
16 Waterloo Place
Edinburgh EH1 3DN

Tel: 031-556 8400 ext 3878
GTN: 2688 3878

Her Majesty's Stationery Office

HMSO (Personnel Services Division)
Sovereign House
Botolph Street
Norwich NR3 1DN

Tel: 0603 694201
GTN: 2014 4201

Department of Trade and Industry

Department of Trade and Industry
Management Services and Manpower Division
Room 423
29 Bressendon Place
London SW1E 5DT

Tel: 01-215 3650
GTN: 215 3650

HM Treasury

Chessington Computer Centre
Government Buildings
Leatherhead Road
Chessington
Surrey KT9 2LT

Tel: 01-391 3800
GTN: 2520 3800

appendix
who's who in the
civil service — a
guide to grades

There are dozens of individual grades and occupational groups within the Civil Service. Some of them are referred to in the examples in this book. The ones you are most likely to come across cover the *administration group* — in effect the non-specialist core of the non-industrial Civil Service — and the senior management grades from all disciplines, which now form the *unified structure*, eg higher management grades from the Science and Professional and Technology Groups. The numbered *unified grades* may be more familiar to many readers under their administration group names — Principal, Assistant Secretary, and so on.

Administrative Assistant	the lower of the two grades of administrative/clerical support
Administrative Officer	the higher of the two grades of administrative/clerical support
Executive Officer (EO)	the junior or first line manager grade
Higher Executive Officer (HEO)	the lower of the two grades of middle management
Senior Executive Officer (SEO)	the higher of the two grades of middle management

Grade 7 (includes Principal and equivalent grades from the old categorisation)	lowest of the higher management grades
Grade 6 (includes Senior Principal and equivalents)	as the former name implies, a grade with more management responsibility
Grade 5 (includes Assistant Secretary and equivalents)	highest of the higher management grades: in Whitehall typically in charge of major policy areas
Grade 4	comparatively rare; manager of a number of Grade 5 post holders
Grade 3 (includes Under Secretary)	lower of two grades of the most senior managers
Grade 2 (includes Deputy Secretary)	higher of two grades of the most senior managers
Grade 1 (Permanent Secretary)	top of the senior management structure; head of main government department

Printed in the United Kingdom for Her Majesty's Stationery Office.
Dd 289882, 10/87, C30, 434, 5673.